Back to the Wild

Keith West

Text © Keith West 2003

The right of Keith West to be identified as the author of this work has been asserted by him in accordance with the Copyright, Designs and Patents Act 1988.

All rights reserved. No part of this publication may be reproduced or transmitted in any form or by any means, electronic or mechanical, including photocopy, recording or any information storage and retrieval system, without permission in writing from the publisher or under licence from the Copyright Licensing Agency Limited, 90 Tottenham Court Road, London W1T 4LP.

Any person who commits any unauthorised act in relation to this publication may be liable to criminal prosecution and civil claims for damages.

Published in 2003 by:
Nelson Thornes Ltd
Delta Place
27 Bath Road
CHELTENHAM
GL53 7TH
United Kingdom

03 04 05 06 07 / 10 9 8 7 6 5 4 3 2 1

A catalogue record for this book is available from the British Library

ISBN 0 7487 7245 6

Cover illustration by Tomas Bjornsson
Page make-up by Tech-Set, Gateshead

Printed in Croatia by Zrinski

1

Africa, 1988

That year there were many elephants in Africa. They trampled down fences and ate crops belonging to the tribesmen. The tribesmen wanted something done about it. They'd heard of a hunter called Buck, so the chief sent for him. Would he kill the elephants that were eating their crops?

Buck agreed. He got together some men. Soon their trucks were bumping along the dusty road. As they drew near the elephants, Buck gave the order to shoot. The crack of rifle fire rang through the jungle.

Panic took hold of the herd as it tried to escape. An old elephant fell to the ground. The other elephants bellowed with fear. There were more shots and more elephants were killed. They crashed down on top of each other.

One small elephant kept close to its mother. Buck saw it was trying to stop itself from being hit. He put down his rifle and ordered his men to do the same.

Buck approached the mother elephant's body. It lay still on the ground. He pulled the baby elephant from under its mother and tied it up. But the mother was only wounded.

She knew what was happening. She got to her feet and ran at the men. She put her trunk around one man and stabbed at him with her tusks. The hunter cried out in pain.

Another hunter ran towards the angry elephant. He shot her between the eyes and she sank to the ground. But the young elephant wasn't hurt. Buck ordered his men to put it into his truck.

The young elephant cried out. But no other elephant answered its call. It pushed its trunk out of a slit in the truck. It tried to smell the scent of other elephants. But all it could smell was death.

Buck started the truck. He was tired and had a long drive back home. He'd done as the chief asked but he hadn't enjoyed the killing.

Night fell and Buck drove on. In the darkness he saw another herd of elephants. The small elephant in the back of the truck cried out to them. The herd bellowed and pushed against the vehicle. They were trying to turn it over. Buck held tight to the wheel. He felt as if he was on a rocking horse.

He jammed the truck in gear and it shot forward through the herd. The elephants butted it as it went past. They were trying to rescue the baby. Should he let the elephant go? He might die if the truck rolled over. He had to think fast.

Quickly, he turned on all the truck's lights. He knew elephants were afraid of lights at night. Bellowing, the elephants fled into the darkness. Buck breathed a sigh of relief. His idea had paid off. He was a lucky man!

Some hours later, Buck reached his ranch. He called to his wife, Rita.

'I've brought you a present.'

2

The elephant was female. Buck and his wife called her Amy. Rita had to get Amy to eat. To begin with she fed her boiled rice mixed with milk powder. She put Amy's trunk into a bucket of warm milk. The elephant learned to suck up the milk with her trunk. Rita then put the trunk into Amy's mouth. She needed to learn how to drink like an adult elephant.

Once she'd mastered it, Amy drank a beaker of milk every ten minutes. She needed feeding 24 hours a day. It was hard work and Rita soon got tired of it.

'You'll have to sell Amy,' she said to Buck. 'I can't cope any longer.'

So Buck got a man to come and look at the elephant. He told Buck he wanted to buy Amy and sell her to a circus in America. Buck had saved Amy and he didn't like the idea of her going to the circus. He'd given her a good life. But he couldn't keep the elephant any longer. He had to sell her.

Amy was put on a plane with five other small African elephants heading for America. They had a keeper with them. His job was to feed them and to see they didn't get sick. Sometimes he talked to them to keep them calm.

He did his work well. All the elephants but Amy had a safe trip. The memory of her herd being shot was still fresh in her mind. She felt afraid and went off her food. She was lucky to be alive when the plane reached America.

3

America

Bob Norris was a cowboy. He kept cows and other animals on his ranch. He loved looking after animals. While Amy was on her way to America, Bob was thinking about a pet bear he'd had as a boy. The bear had lost both its parents, so he'd reared it. He'd called it Lulu. Bob and Lulu had gone everywhere together. They'd eaten ice cream and honey on the ranch. They were the best of friends. To Bob, Lulu was part of the family.

But the black bear had grown big and strong. She could snap a steel chain like snapping a twig. She went all over the farm and did as she liked. Bob's dad thought Lulu might hurt somebody by mistake. If this happened she'd have to be shot and Bob's father would be in trouble.

Bob knew the bear wouldn't hurt anyone. He wanted Lulu to wander free. But the neighbours were afraid. They called the sheriff. He came to see Bob's dad and told him Lulu should go to a zoo.

When Bob came home from school one day he couldn't find the bear. His dad told him what the sheriff had said. Bob was upset. He knew Lulu wouldn't harm anyone. He knew she wasn't dangerous. Now it was too late to do anything about it.

There and then he made a vow. He'd never let another pet go to a zoo. He couldn't bear the thought of animals being shut up in cages. He believed they should be free to roam as they did in the wild.

He'd been too late to save Lulu. But he wasn't too late to save other animals. Like the lambs which were born on trains carrying sheep to market. If a railroad man found a newborn lamb, he took it from its mother and threw it on to the road next to the track.

Bob used to go to the rail yards and watch the trains arrive. The railroad bosses kept an eye open. They didn't like boys in their yard. If boys were caught near the trucks, they'd get a good beating.

He used to hide and watch the railroad men at work. He hated it when the men threw the lambs on to the road. When the trains had left, he'd pick up the lambs and run home with them. Some of the lambs died, but many more of them lived.

Bob never forgot the vow he'd made as a boy. He loved animals, but he wanted them to be free. He decided to become a cowboy with his own ranch.

4

The years passed. Bob worked for ranchers who knew all about animals. Then he became a cowboy himself, like he'd always wanted to be. But a cowboy's life doesn't always go to plan.

One day he was alone with his horse, checking fences. It was the middle of winter and the weather was freezing. He had to break ice from waterholes so the animals could drink. As he worked, a blizzard blew in from the north. It wasn't long before everywhere was covered in snow. The wind pushed the snow into Bob's eyes and ears. Icy splinters scratched his skin.

All Bob could see was a blanket of snow stretching into the distance. He knew he was lost and in deep trouble. He thought he'd freeze to death. He dropped the horse's reins. He talked to it and asked it to take him home. The horse seemed to understand. It began to plod through the snow.

Soon, Bob's hands were frozen. He pulled his jacket tightly around himself. He pulled his cowboy hat down almost to his eyes. His feet felt like stones. His eyebrows were thick with ice. He was sure his horse was going the wrong way. But it was his only hope. He had no idea which way to go. He had to trust it.

Hours passed by. The weather grew worse. The snow blew in deep drifts across the hills. He could see nothing but a white land under a white sky. He was sure he was going to die.

At last, the horse stopped. Bob was so weak he didn't know what was happening. He pushed up the brim of his hat. He could hear the ice cracking all around. Then a wonderful sight met his eyes. It was his ranch. His horse had brought him home.

Bob remembered his black bear, Lulu. He'd trusted Lulu with his life. Now, years later, his horse had saved his life. His love of animals had paid off.

5

Bob married and had children of his own. He loved his life as a cowboy. He was a lucky man. Not only was he doing a job he enjoyed, but he was working with animals too. He liked working with horses best. He loved riding across the prairie and rounding up the cattle. He was such a good cowboy he was asked to be in adverts on TV. For 12 years his picture was shown on American television. People thought he was the perfect cowboy.

Not long after his spell of fame, Bob met Amy. This is how it happened. One morning, he saw a stranger on his ranch. Bob asked the man what he wanted. The stranger said his name was Jackson. He said he was looking for horse stalls to rent. Bob told him he didn't rent out stalls.

'I don't want the stalls for horses,' Jackson told him. 'I want them for elephants.'

Bob was surprised. 'Elephants?'

'Yeah. Young elephants. Not too big yet. I need somewhere safe until they're sold.'

'Do you have a buyer?' Bob asked.

'Not yet. Someone'll have them. A zoo, a circus maybe. Or I can split them up.'

At first, Bob wasn't too happy about the idea. But in the end he agreed to let the man rent some stalls. He'd looked after horses, cows and a black bear. But it would be the first time he'd had elephants on the ranch.

The next day, the elephants arrived in the back of a truck. They were still small enough to fit into the stalls. Before he drove away, Jackson left them some food. Bob watched as four of the elephants ate hungrily. But one wouldn't eat. She just sniffed her food and walked away. The elephant was Amy.

Bob had learned to understand the ways of animals. Right away, he knew Amy was too frightened to eat. He was worried. Over the next few days he spent time with her. She got used to his voice. He helped her eat some oats and drink some milk. He noticed she was the smallest of the elephants. She was quiet and the other elephants bullied her. He wondered why.

At that time, he knew nothing of her life in Africa.

6

One lunch break, Bob was sitting on a fence on his ranch watching the young elephants. His eyes were on Amy. She was the smallest elephant he'd ever seen. He noticed how the others pushed her away from the food. This upset him.

While Jackson was away, Bob kept trying to get the timid elephant to eat. She took a few oats but it wasn't enough to keep her fit. When Jackson came back, he told Bob that Amy was not putting on weight like the other elephants. Something was wrong.

Bob tried to make Amy feel less nervous. He'd heard that elephants like carrots, so one day he cut up a carrot and gave her a slice. After a time she ate it and held up her trunk for more. He was making progress, but it was slow. It was then he noticed something else about Amy. She never left her stall. She was afraid of open spaces. He decided to keep the stall door open to see what she would do.

For a long time, Amy stayed inside. Then, one day, she left her stall. She walked slowly into the paddock and lifted her trunk to smell the air. Then one of the cowboys on horseback came riding towards her and made her afraid again. She ran back inside.

The other elephants were afraid of the horses on the ranch too. They kept close together for safety, leaving Amy on her own. They sensed she was different. They hit her with their trunks and stole her food. Bob often rode into the paddock and frightened them off. He spent time with Amy, trying to get her to eat and drink. He felt she was starting to trust him. It seemed as if she knew he wanted to help her.

One day, Jackson came to the ranch and went to the stalls. He was in a bad mood. Bob watched him chase Amy. He hit her with a board when she wouldn't do as he wanted. This made Bob very angry. He'd put in a lot of hard work to make the elephant less afraid of humans. Bob ran across to Jackson and grabbed the board from him. He threw it on to the ground. Bob's eyes were ablaze with anger as he faced Jackson.

'Never let me see you touch her again,' he shouted.

Jackson knew Bob meant what he said. Jackson got in his truck and drove off. A few days later, he came back. He was in a better mood. He explained to Bob how Amy's herd had been killed in Africa and how Buck had saved her life. He spoke about the long plane journey to America.

Bob began to understand Amy better. He knew she must have bad memories of the shooting. He knew she'd never had happy times. He had to try to teach her to forget the past.

He'd learnt to tell the signs that Amy was unhappy. She hit the walls of her stall with her trunk. He never heard her make a sound. Silent elephants are sick elephants. He didn't want her to be sick. He wanted her to become a part of his family of animals. He wanted her to get well.

He knew Amy needed a reason to live. He remembered a story about a pair of llamas that had escaped from a zoo. The police shot the male Llama dead. A little later, the female grew so upset she died too. Bob didn't want Amy to pine away like that.

He called a vet to check her for illness. The vet thought there was nothing badly wrong. She told Bob that Amy needed to be shown kindness. Bob thought he'd look after her and show her kindness.

7

After a time, Jackson sold most of the elephants. Some went to zoos and others went to circuses. But he couldn't find a home for Amy. She stood alone in the paddock.

One Saturday, as Bob stood by her stall, Jackson told him he'd found a buyer for Amy. A woman was going to collect her later that week. The woman kept all kinds of strange pets. She had tigers, lions and even snakes. Bob was worried because he thought the woman might treat Amy badly. Then a thought struck him. He asked Jackson if he could buy the elephant instead. Jackson agreed. When he left the ranch, he had Bob's money in his pocket.

The weeks passed and Bob wondered if he'd done the right thing. He didn't know much about elephants. Could he look after Amy and give her a good life? But he did know one thing. Animals need friends. He wondered if Amy would make friends with the other animals on the ranch.

As Bob stood by the stalls, he saw two dogs playing with a ball. It was too big for them to pick up. They knocked the ball with their legs. Amy watched the dogs from the corner of the paddock. They left her alone.

One of the dogs was called Butch. When the other dog got sick, Butch was on his own. He kicked the ball towards Amy. She got the idea and hit it with her trunk. It rolled against the stall door. Then she kicked the ball and it rolled to Butch. The dog fell over the ball and it rolled to Amy. She began to chase it across the paddock.

Now Butch forgot the ball and chased the elephant's trunk instead. Amy spun around. Butch could never catch her trunk. It seemed the elephant had found a friend at last.

Bob was cleaning saddles and ropes when he heard a noise like a trumpet. He pushed his hat back and watched. Amy was chasing Butch around the paddock. She let out another blast of sound. She couldn't believe she'd made the noise herself. Bob laughed. He knew Amy would be much happier now she'd made a friend.

For a time it seemed as if Amy was on the mend. But it didn't last. When the other dog got better, Butch played with him instead.

8

As Bob watched Amy one day, a mouse ran into her stall. The elephant had scooped some grain into a tiny pile. The mouse began to eat the grain. Bob wondered if the elephant had left food for the mouse so it would visit her. He felt sorry for Amy. She needed a better friend than Butch and a bigger friend than a mouse.

There was a goat on the farm called Michelle. Bob decided to put her in a field near Amy. After a time, the elephant and the goat became friends. Amy liked to wrap her trunk around Michelle. The goat didn't seem to notice Amy was an elephant.

But the friendship didn't last. The goat often ate junk from the scrap bin and chewed rubber mats. But one day she ate some of the grain Amy had put by for the mouse. Amy put her trunk around Michelle's middle and pulled the goat away.

The other goat on the ranch was called Larry. He tried to butt Amy, so she hit him with her trunk. His feet left the ground. He wasn't badly hurt but he'd come off worse.

One afternoon Bob was walking past Amy's stall. He heard the male goat grunting. The young elephant had pinned Larry against the wall. She was pushing him with her head. She could have killed him. Bob didn't want Amy to kill another animal. He shouted at her and she let Larry go. After that, the goat kept away from her. Amy was alone again.

The elephant was growing fast. Bob's wife was worried Amy might hurt somebody. By this time she was getting up to tricks. She'd learned to undo the bolts on her stall and turn on the water tap. She was getting clever and strong. Bob and his wife were afraid she might even be dangerous.

Bob saw she had to be trained.

9

One day Bob's daughter, Carole, was watching a TV programme. It said that a lot of people were killed by elephants. If you trained them properly they were gentle animals. The programme showed a man called Maguire training elephants. He was working with a big male elephant. The elephant was once wild but Maguire told it to lie down. He only had to ask once. The elephant did as it was told. Maybe Amy could be trained too.

Carole phoned the TV station and asked to speak to Maguire. She explained the problem with their elephant. She asked if he could help her father train Amy. Maguire thought she was joking. He couldn't believe he was speaking to someone whose father owned an elephant. He said he only trained elephants in zoos and circuses. But he'd take a look at her. Maybe he could help.

Maguire was good at his job. He'd trained all kinds of animals. He'd trained lions and tigers, but he liked to work with elephants best. He knew they could be trained to do as they were told.

There was only one snag. Amy's training would cost a lot of money. But Bob felt the money was worth spending. He knew Amy had to be trained. He knew Maguire could do it. He didn't want her to hurt anyone. It couldn't wait. Bob knew young animals were the easiest to train. He only hoped she wasn't too old.

10

Maguire soon saw Amy's problem. Bob had spoiled her. Now she thought she could do whatever she wanted. Bob had been so kind to her she didn't take orders. If she was going to be safe with people, Maguire would have to train her. Quickly.

He had a long stick. He tied Amy's legs with a rope. He looped the rope around her neck. Amy hated the rope. She tried to fight against it. But Maguire didn't mean any harm. He gave her treats if she did well. He tapped her with his stick if she did badly. He gave Amy the order to lie down. At first, she was afraid. But she soon knew she wasn't going to be hurt. She lay down.

Amy was clever. She got to know what Maguire wanted her to do. He taught her to raise her trunk and lift her leg. She was given a biscuit each time as a reward.

'I'll never send Amy to a zoo,' said Bob. 'She'll stay on the ranch when you've trained her.'

Maguire smiled and nodded. 'I know that, Bob. Don't worry. Amy will be fine.'

It took a long time. In the end, Maguire's hard work paid off. He'd taught Amy to obey him. He'd also taught her to obey Bob. To prove she was trained, he asked a local school to watch her. All the children came to the ranch. Bob dressed in a cowboy outfit.

Amy knew something was happening. She knew she had to do as she was asked. She skipped for Bob and waved a little American flag with her trunk. She stood to attention. But when Bob asked her to take a nap, she just walked away. Bob was worried. Amy hadn't done as he asked. He felt he'd failed.

But Amy hadn't forgotten. She turned and came back. She lay at Bob's feet and took her nap.

Bob gave Amy a pat. He took a biscuit from his pocket and popped it in her mouth. He put a ribbon around her neck to show she'd passed her test. She was fully trained. Now Amy was happy. And safe.

11

The years passed. Amy was six years old. She weighed over 1,000 kilos and stood two metres high. African elephants never stop growing.

Bob's wife, Jane, was watching TV news one night. A zoo keeper had hit an elephant with a stick. The elephant had snatched the stick from his hands and thrown him in the air. He'd fallen on a steel fence and hurt his back. Jane didn't want that to happen to her husband. She told him about the zoo keeper as soon as he got home.

'But he hit the elephant,' said Bob. 'I'd never hit Amy. Anyway, it's not only elephants that hurt people. Horses can hurt people too. I've never been hurt by a horse. But I've never hit one with a stick either!'

Jane wasn't so sure. She knew Amy had been trained, but she felt the elephant was getting too big for the ranch.

Shortly after, Bob's son was helping on the ranch. He was in Amy's stall. She pushed him against the wall. Luckily, Bob saw and shouted at Amy and she stopped pushing. What might have happened if Bob hadn't been there? Perhaps his son would have been killed. Bob remembered what his wife had said about the keeper. Was she right about Amy?

There was something else. Elephants live a long time. Amy might be alive after Bob's death. What would happen to her then? She was getting stronger every day. Bob had to face facts. Amy would have to go. Just like Lulu years before.

12

A man called Buckles owned a circus. One afternoon he got a phone call from Maguire. He told Buckles about Bob's African elephant. The elephant had got too big for Bob's ranch.

Buckles thought African elephants were hard to train for the circus. Asian elephants were easier. But his wife, Barbara, went to see Amy. Maguire showed Barbara how well trained the elephant was. Barbara thought the elephant would be good for the circus and told her husband to take her.

At first, Bob didn't want Amy to go. She'd spent most of her life on the ranch. She'd got used to Bob's ways. Would she survive in a circus? He'd have to hope that Buckles knew what he was doing. When they came to pick Amy up, Bob walked away and didn't look back.

Barbara put two elephants, Anna May and Ned, in a field with Amy. She thought the elephants would be friends. Amy's world had suddenly changed again. Everything was strange. She'd got used to Bob's ranch. This new place frightened her.

That night Amy heard the sounds of the other elephants. She'd not heard other elephants since she was a baby in

Africa. Were the hunters coming again to shoot the herd? She stayed in her stall and beat the walls with her trunk.

Over the next week, she wouldn't eat or move. She began to lose weight again. She was pining for Bob. Bob felt the same. He rode his horse and did his jobs on the ranch. But his mind wasn't on horses. He was thinking about Amy.

Weeks passed. One day Ned rolled a tyre to Amy. She had no interest. She let it go by. Ned tried again and, little by little, she joined in the game. Amy was good at rolling the tyre but Ned was not so clever. She began to tease him. She took the tyre from him and he couldn't get it back. Amy even teased Ned as he slept. She kept poking him with her trunk so he had no peace.

But things were different between Amy and Anna May. They called to each other and held trunks. Amy began to follow Anna May around. She ate when Anna May ate. Everything Anna May did, Amy did. This time she'd found a real friend. She began to put on weight. Buckles knew she'd survive circus life.

Maguire had already trained Amy to obey orders. Now Buckles had to train her for the circus. The circus ring was her new life. She soon learned to do as was asked. She learned to lift a big basket in her mouth. In the basket was Buckles's granddaughter, Skye.

Then the elephants were taught to hold each other's tails. They skipped around the ring in time to music. Amy had been taught to skip a half beat behind the other elephants. The crowd laughed. Then she stole popcorn from the boys in the front row. The crowd always gave her a big clap.

Sometimes Amy got bored. She'd leave the ring and go back to her stall. She was clever but she didn't always do as she was told. The crowd thought it was part of her act. Buckles didn't let on.

A year passed and Bob couldn't stop worrying what Amy was doing. He decided to visit the circus. He thought Amy wouldn't remember him. He knew the food she liked so he bought some buns. He also brought along some carrots and strawberries in chocolate. He sat on the front row. The band began to play. The lights went down. The animals came into the ring.

Amy was the fourth elephant to enter. She held Anna May's tail. The elephants danced around the ring. Amy didn't seem to notice Bob. He thought she'd forgotten him.

Just then, Amy dropped Anna May's tail. She trumpeted and turned to Bob's seat. She raced around the ring and stopped in front of him. She sank to her knees, and laid her head in Bob's lap. She'd remembered him.

The crowd thought it was part of the act. They clapped and cheered for a long time. They knew nothing about Bob and Amy's story.

Now he needn't worry any more about the elephant. She'd got used to the life of the circus.

But, shortly after, something bad happened. Buckles came to see Bob on his ranch. He looked worried. They talked about the circus and the elephants.

'There's something I have to tell you,' said Buckles.

'What?' asked Bob.

'You'll have to find Amy a new home. The doctor's told Barbara she can't work again. And I'm getting too old for circus life. You'll have to find another home for the elephant.'

13

Bob was very sad. In her short life Amy had had so many homes and friends. How would she cope with another change? This was not a good life for the elephant. Bob had to think of something.

Bob had heard of a man named Randall. Randall had taken elephants back to Africa. He was looking for more elephants to take back. He wanted them to go back to the wild. Bob phoned him and told him about Amy. He told Randall that Buckles was leaving the circus in a year's time.

'Don't worry,' Randall told him. 'I'll take care of Amy.'

Bob trusted Randall. He knew he was as good as his word.

Amy was now old enough to have a mate. She needed to live with a herd and have her own babies. All this could happen in Africa. And that is where she went. Randall took her back to where she was born. She was taken to Africa to spend the rest of her life with other elephants. She'd be safe, back where she was born.

Bob is now old. He still works on his ranch and rides his horses. He still loves animals and remembers Amy with fondness. He's glad she's back in Africa.

He'll never see her again. But he knows Africa is where she belongs.

The end

This story was inspired by *The Cowboy and his Elephant* by Malcolm MacPherson (Headline Book Publishing, 2001).